Page One

Teresa,

Thank you for letting
me be a part
of your family.

Mick

Page One
Two Truths Guaranteed to Change Your Life Forever from the
First Page of the Bible

Mick Thornton

For those who are empty,
and the One who sent His Son to fill them.

CONTENTS

Introduction: Full and Empty   1

The First Truth

1   Two Questions   11

2   Change   15

3   In The Beginning   17

4   The Big Reveal   21

5   Priorities   25

6   Disorder   29

7   Order   33

8   The Two Categories   37

9   Because God is First, Your Life Has Order   45

10 Because God is First, You Are Free   49

11 Because God is First, You Have Clarity   51

12 Because God is First, Nothing Else Is   55

The Second Truth

13	Everything Else	63
14	Back to the Mountain	69
15	Spoiler Alert	73
16	Image and Apex	77
17	Creators and Credit	81
18	Second	85
19	Craving Greatness	87
20	Because People Are Second, People Are Great	93
21	Because People Are Second, You Have an Identity	95
22	Because People Are Second, You Have a Job to Do	101
23	Because You Are Second, You Matter	107
24	Because People Are Second, We Are All Equal	109
25	Because We Are Second, We Have Someone to Thank	113
26	Because We Are Second, We Have Zero Cause for Arrogance	117
27	Because We Are Second, We Can Worship	121

The Forever-Changed Life

28	The End of the Quest	129
29	The New Quest	133
30	The Fizzle that Started the Frazzle	135
31	Turning the Page	139
32	The Next Mountain	143
33	The New Today	147

| Thank You | 155 |
| About The Author | 159 |

FULL AND EMPTY

The Bible is a thick book. In fact, it's an ancient collection of 66 different books written over a period of 1,500 years in two different languages. There is a lot going on in there.

Yet, it just sits there. Profound, heavy, and thick.

Meanwhile, our smartphones are very thin. They are an ultramodern combination of touch screen viewing technology and wireless connectivity driven by a tiny computer of almost incomprehensible processing power.

And they are loud.

I have no memory of the day I received my first Bible, but I vividly remember the day that I got my first smartphone. It felt very nearly like a holy moment. I opened the magnificent packaging, then gently cradled a device in my hands that promised to be the answer to my problems. I had every expectation that this little wonder of modern technology was going to be the key to streamlining my life.

No longer would I be missing meetings or forgetting to take out the trash. Over were the days of being disconnected from the world. No longer would I miss vital information because it was sent to me via social media rather than email, text message, voicemail, or whatever new way the world was communicating that week. With this flat-screened wonder, I would walk boldly into a new era of life—always on time, always in the know, always in touch.

I could not have been more excited.

We live in a world where about a thousand different things are all clamoring for our attention all at the same time. Door bells ring, traffic lights turn, horns honk, people talk, kids scream, the television blares, phones ding, smart watches buzz, all of it demanding the exact same thing:

us.

So we give it. A piece of us here, a piece of us

there, until there is nothing more to give. Yet the ringing and turning and honking and talking and screaming and blaring and dinging and buzzing continues.

It's no wonder that we're frazzled. We weren't built for this.

In fact, we actually had to invent that word—frazzled—to explain this feeling. It's a combination of two older words that means we are wearing out and coming apart, both at the same time. **For many of us, there could not be a more accurate word to describe our lives.**

But for me, in that first moment when I powered-on my first smartphone, I honestly believed that I had found the solution to all my frazzle.

I was wrong.

At some point, a software engineer decided that it would be a good idea to place a small red circle with a number in it next to every application icon on my phone when it wanted to tell me something. The more "notifications" that particular app wants to give me, the higher the number. I discovered quickly that it was important to disable notifications on every non-essential app.

Regardless, as I write these words, I have no less than 765 notifications on my phone. That's 765 emails, text messages, voice messages, reminders, social media updates, weather alerts, software updates, calendar appointments, plus a few other things.

Make that 766.

I call them red dots of failure. My phone looks as if all of the people whom I am currently failing in 766 (now 767) different ways became a pitchfork-wielding mob and attacked the one device guaranteed to always be in my possession.

This miracle device that was supposed to un-frazzle my life has become a constantly beeping, buzzing, dinging reminder that my life is unlivable, doomed to seep red, unceasing failure. And each time I pick up my phone to write a note or make a reminder or send a message, I'm confronted by a host of notifications that need my immediate attention. I take care of one, don't have time for the second, then I can't remember why I picked up my phone in the first place!

But sitting quietly somewhere in the midst of all the frazzle there is this old book. The Bible.

In our click-bait world, the Bible feels like a dinosaur. In the Bible, you will not find chapters or books entitled, "Five Easy Steps to a Whole New You," or "Three Choices that Every Successful Person Must Make." Instead, you find books with names like Deuteronomy and Third John, and chapter headings like, "A Lament and Call to Repentance" and "Paul's Vision of a Man from Macedonia."

And it never dings.

The fact is that in a world where so many things are calling constantly for our attention, an ancient collection of books seems starkly out of place.

But let's just say that in this world of immediate everything, you have discovered a problem. Let's just say that you have discovered that *you* are out of place. You wake up every morning, you go to sleep at night (or vice versa), and your moments in between always seem to be full. And yet you are not full.

To the contrary, you are empty.

You are one of the billions of people in the world today whose full days leave you hollow. So you try to fill the void. You eat too much, then you diet. You drink too much, then you abstain. You work too much, then you quit. You buy too much, then you sell it. You love too much, then you lose it.

Wherever you find yourself in the binge-and-purge cycle of life, it's not working. Your life changes a little, the blogs you read and shows you watch change a lot, but you are still empty. So you grab hold of the next ticket to the good life that comes dinging or buzzing or flashing your way.

But somewhere deep inside of you there is this inescapable whisper reminding you that last month's ticket to the good life didn't pan out, and this month's ticket to the good life isn't panning out, and the next ticket that comes along isn't going to pan out either. But you click on it anyway, because that is what we do.

Or maybe you don't.

Maybe in the midst of all of the fleeting, noisy bustle of life, you find yourself looking for something that is less flashy and more enduring. Something that a life can be built on rather than filled with. Maybe you find yourself looking for the kind of thing that, with great effort, a person might discover somewhere deep within the confines of a thick, dusty, ancient book.

Good news for you. When you crack open that Bible, not only are you are going to find the life that you have been looking for, you are going to find it on the *first page*.

And I'm going to help you do it.

But be forewarned. If you want to keep thinking of yourself in the way you do now, keep thinking of your life in the way you do now, and keep feeling how you feel now, stop now. Go click on something.

In fact, go click on lots of things. All that noise is your only hope if you want to keep living a life that is full on the outside and empty on the inside. If you want that life, you *need* all of that noise. Desperately.

But if you are ready for a life whose fullness flows from the inside out, then you are ready for Page One.

So here we go.

THE FIRST TRUTH

TWO QUESTIONS

I t was a dark and stormy night. Only this storm was not blowing from west to east across the endless desert sky. This storm was raging directly on top of a mountain. And our idiot leader was up there and probably dead.

If you want to understand the first page of the Bible, this is as good a place to start as any. Because this is exactly the situation in life of the first people to ever read it.

They were a nation of slaves. It was all they had ever known for longer than anyone could remember. Then a celebrity leader showed up. That's when all the trouble started.

His name was Moses. He was born during a time when the slave masters of ancient Egypt decided that there were too many of their own personal slave nation, the Israelites. So the Pharaoh demanded that every newborn baby boy must be thrown into the river to die. But in an act of glorious rebellion, Moses' mother hid him. Then she secretly placed him in a tiny boat and cast him off so that he would float down the river directly to the place where the king's daughter was.

The plan worked. The king's daughter saw Moses, saved him, and raised him like an orphaned puppy in the house of the king.

Life went on. It does that.

Moses grew up. He dealt badly with the experience of watching his adopted family enslave his biological people, and eventually he ran away to a different life for a long time. But then he came back, with a God-given vengeance.

He marched into the palace, claimed that the god of his people is actually the God of everything, and that HE, the LORD God, demands the freedom of His people. Then Moses called down from heaven one horror after another until the king of the most powerful nation on the planet actually agreed to let the slave people go.

It was a rocky departure, to say the least, but several days later, the people found themselves gathered up around this desert mountain. God revealed His presence as a raging storm, Moses went up into the storm, and all the people down below were scared, bored, and questioning their life choices.

And while a God-storm raging on a desert mountain might be a little bit outside of your life experiences, I'll bet that you know that other part really well.

Most people have found themselves scared, bored, and questioning their life choices. In fact, many people find themselves right there right now. Maybe you are one of them.

From there, the first page of the Bible starts to make a lot of sense.

It should. Because it was at the base of that mountain that God gave His people the first page and the first book of the Bible.

The base of that mountain. With Moses nowhere in sight for days upon days. As fear and boredom distilled into anger and regret. As livestock moaned and kids fought and played. As adults stared and tried not to stare at the storming mountain.

At the base of that mountain, two questions had to be ringing, beeping, and buzzing their way through that whole group of people:

Who is God? and Who are we?

CHANGE

Fun fact about people: we don't like change.

In fact, people are so skin-crawlingly uncomfortable with change that even when a person is removed from a terrible situation very often that person will either return to it or re-create it elsewhere. In fact, maybe that is your story today. Maybe you know that impulse well.

It was exactly that impulse that took hold in the slave nation before Moses eventually came down from the raging mountain. They had tasted freedom, they had even glimpsed God, and their ultimate conclusion was that it was—different. So they were well on their way to either skulking back into their miserable slavery, or finding a way to re-create it elsewhere.

If they were going to walk into this new life, they needed a darn good reason, and they needed it fast.

Maybe so do you. After all, with every second that you spend reading these words, your life is calling you. And it is not calling you forward. It's calling you back.

IN THE BEGINNING

For the slave nation, their pressing questions were, "Who is God?" and "Who are we?" For most of us, our questions seem to be a little more practical than those.

They aren't.

We are about to discover that these two questions are the most practical and important questions that can ever be asked because the way that you answer them changes everything.

You don't have to believe that yet. But stick with me and I think you will.

Page one of the Bible starts with some of the

most famous words ever written. Words that in our modern world have been printed in more languages than any other. In fact, these are the first words ever to be printed after the invention of the printing press.

In the beginning God created the heavens and the earth. ~Genesis 1:1

In one of the great ironies of existence, doesn't that feel just a bit anticlimactic? Here we are with places to go, people to see, things to do, and an emptiness inside of us that echoes so loudly that we are driven to seek out and consider the terrible possibility of an utterly new life. And our hope is to be found in a history lesson?

In a word: Yep.

Most of us are not cosmologists. We have neither the time nor the interest to think deeply about the cosmic question of where we came from. Between the regrets of yesterday and the fears of tomorrow lies the fullness of today. So the chances of us taking a moment of today, wrestling it away from tomorrow or yesterday, and using it to think about the *first* day are not good.

Generally speaking we are more likely to focus on cosmetology than cosmology. We are more likely to invest in decorating *who* we are than in discovering *why* we are.

Which is exactly why we are so empty.

On the title page of this little textual adventure, I promised you two truths that would change your life. Here is the first one:

God is first.

THE BIG REVEAL

God is first. He is for real, and He is glorious.
When God has visibly orchestrated the destruction of your old miserable life in Egypt, then visibly walked you through the Red Sea and towards your new life, His identity seems very relevant. Especially when He is visibly present, actively guiding you to where you should and shouldn't go.

But when God is reduced to a word people use at weddings, funerals, and in particularly passionate curses, He seems less relevant. Especially when His presence seems to be vastly less noticeable in your average day than Amazon or Google.

But what if God is still Himself? What if this

entire extravaganza that we call life is happening because He invented it? What if He is just as active in the world now as He has ever been?

If all of that is true, then the identity of this God continues to be very relevant. In fact, it is the most relevant fact in the universe.

Take a second and notice something for me. Notice the device upon which you are reading these words. Most likely it's a computer, tablet, phone, or e-reader. It is made of a long list of exotic materials, and there is not one person on planet Earth who actually knows how to make it. It is the result of a massive collective effort of people and production equipment. Each played a part in its conception, design, and creation. And not a single one of them has the ability to go back and create from basic elements the product you are using.

Now take a step back from there. All of those people came from other people (their parents), who came from other people (*their* parents). All of the technology was a development that came from previous developments. And every material used came from somewhere on planet Earth.

Now take a step back from there.

The claim of the first sentence of the first page of the Bible is that the ultimate source or origin of everything required for your device to exist, is God. In fact, the fact that *anything* exists is proof of nothing less than God. Not because any of those things *is* God. Because everything came from somewhere. And that somewhere, ultimately, is Him.

God is first. He is the un-created Creator.

That's important, because if you are going to move forward from empty to full in your life, you need a reason that is powerful, true, and real. Without that reason, you are like a child in paper wings jumping off a roof. The launch may be beautiful, but the landing won't be.

PRIORITIES

The claim that God is the maker of everything has proven remarkably durable over time. Even in our highly advanced era in which science and technology provide us with products and related philosophies that would have been inconceivable even a decade ago, branches of what is called Historical Science still tend to very intentionally avoid the subject of the actual origins of the universe. Even Big Bang cosmologists rarely speculate on the causes or origins of the bang itself. But 3,500 years before hadron colliders, the first page of the Bible states matter-of-factly and unashamedly that the source of all things is God.

Now let's talk for a second about how that changes everything.

All people have priorities. Even when we can't name them, we have them. And the less we can name them, the more they have us.

Directly stated, all people are slaves to our priorities. They give shape to our lives. Our priorities dictate everything from what we eat to who we hate. They are like the pistons inside of the engines of our cars. Most of us almost never think about them, if we even know they exist at all, but without them we would never go anywhere. The fact that you do anything proves that you have priorities.

I want to be happy.

I want to be a good person.

People should be nice to each other.

We should go to the lake this weekend.

Somebody should really fix that pothole.

I'm so hungry I could eat a horse.

All of these are statements of priority. In fact, most everything we say is a statement of priority, and most everything we do is an act of prioritization. There is a sense in which we are best understood as priority robots who are simply following our priority programming as we move through our lives.

So why isn't it working?

If we want what we want, and our wants drive us, why don't we have what we want? Why aren't we all great, amazing people with great, amazing lives that include our own specialized version of a house in the mountains or a sailboat in San Francisco Bay?

The answer is not because we lack priorities. The answer is because our priorities did not make the universe.

DISORDER

O ur lives are out of order. And as long as that is true, our lives will continue to become more and more full, even as we ourselves become more and more empty.

Take this simple statement of priority with which most people would find it easy to agree: I would do anything for my children.

That sounds like the kind of thing that any good parent would say. But any parent who lives out that priority to its fullest is guaranteed to raise rotten kids. Kids who know that someone else will always be there to meet their every want and need, learn to value nothing and no one and become incapable of doing anything but whining for more. To the contrary, rather than doing anything for your children, the wisdom to know what to do and what *not* to do for your children is a hallmark of every good parent.

Any parent who makes it a priority to do anything for their children soon finds themselves with an overwhelming life full of wretched kids and thankless work stretched over the canvas of their empty heart.

Full life, empty you.

Ok, let's try this one: A person is rightly judged by the quality of their work.

That sounds about right. Hard work pays off, so the best lives should belong to those who work the hardest to attain them. Yet in every low-rent trailer park and every exclusive gated suburb, the same story plays out. People work their lives away under the assumption that the next step up the ladder of accomplishment comes with a sense of internal fulfillment that makes it all worth it. The guy working at the tire store thinks life would be grand if only he could become the manager. The lady working at the law firm thinks life would be grand if only she made partner. While the manager and the partners think their lives would be grand if only something else.

Full lives, empty people.

Next try: It's all about the money. Forget hard work or personal integrity, if we could just be filthy stinking rich (or whatever version of that we don't feel guilty about), then comes the good life.

So according to this theory, a lifetime of fulfillment awaits those who get to have everything they want without really having to work for it. If only we were all famous actors or professional athletes or lottery winners or trust fund babies then we would all be practically drowning in personal fulfillment.

I could buy that. But then I hear yet another story of celebrity self-destruction. Another story of a person who is given the world only to find a way to drop it on their own head.

Full lives, empty people.

So let's try for a desperate last shot, shall we? Ultimate altruism: People find ultimate fulfillment through radically serving others. Or more simply stated, I will do anything for anybody.

Replay everything that happened when we tried that with our kids at the beginning of this chapter, only now in every part of your life.

Full life. Empty you.

But here is where it gets really interesting. At least some of the priorities represented in these ideals are at least generally good and generally true, right? So why don't they work? Why do they all yield different versions of the same hollow life?

Because they are out of order.

ORDER

Order matters.

Imagine that your life has taken a definitive turn for the worse. You find yourself in front of a highly trained military firing squad. You stand trembling in terror with a blindfold over your eyes, your hands bound behind your back. Your elbows scratch against a rough and scarred brick wall.

As the smell of death and spent ammunition fills the air, your turn comes. The commander barks out those three fateful words, and you are doomed.

"Ready. Aim. Fire!"

And that's that.

But what if the commander decides to shake things up a bit?

"Ready. Fire. Aim!"

If he keeps that up, you could live a long, if somewhat noisy life.

Order matters.

Instead of the firing squad scenario, let's imagine that you are still your wonderful upstanding self, only you find a lump on the side of your neck. So you go to your family doctor. The doctor pokes and prods you for a few minutes, then makes a diagnosis.

"I don't like this lump. We're going to start immediately with 12 rounds of chemotherapy. Then we're going to follow that with 12 rounds of intense radiation. Then after you recover to the point that you are strong enough to stand and some of your hair starts to grow back, we are going to remove the lump, your lymph nodes, most of your trachea, and probably your right arm just to be safe. "

"Lastly, we will biopsy the lump to see if it was cancer."

Order matters.

In fact, order matters so much that the right things in the wrong order are not the right things. That is the reason why our lives can be full of good things and still empty.

And that is why the Bible starts with God.

In the beginning God created the heavens and the earth.
~Genesis 1:1

The heavens and the Earth equal every created thing. In this sentence we find God, and Everything Else. And the thing we find first is God.

Take note of that. God is first.

THE TWO CATEGORIES

In all of existence, there are essentially two categories of being. There is God. And there is Everything Else. According to the Bible, God comes first by a long shot.

First off, God is forever. Before the beginning, He was already there. Second, God is the maker of Everything Else. He is more important than Everything Else in the same way that an artist is more important than her painting. Thirdly, God is so big and powerful that His making of Everything Else was seemingly effortless.

God goes on to create the entire universe, basically just by talking. To put that in context, God created a trillion stars separated by billions of light years with the same effort that is required for me to order french fries at a drive thru window.

That is an act of first-ness at its finest.

First-ness is not a word. Technically, the word we are looking for is "primacy." And though there is a place in the world for words that most people don't understand, this isn't it. I think that important things should be stated simply. So since this is my book, we're going with first-ness. The attribute of being first.

If we learn anything from the first sentence of the Bible it is that God deserves first-ness.

But as lifetime members of Team Everything Else, it can be hard to get our lives into proper order. As we do laps around our favorite star, we are surrounded by all these other people and things that seem to need our immediate attention most of the time. On top of that we have a mountain of built-in needs and wants of our own. So as a result, it is a very easy thing for our lives to get out of order.

Instead of God being first, something else is given that distinction.

The Two Categories

For most people, first place goes to themselves. Self-focus is the unofficial religion of the modern world. Proudly brought to you by your own broken heart and by everyone who ever wanted to sell you something. There is a world full of opportunities for those whose first priority is to give themselves a better today. The only problem is that every single one of them will eventually fail you because they are all built upon a foundation of a dis-ordered life. Ironically, those who serve themselves most experience fullness the least.

The next popular choice for a disordered life is a life in which one or more other people are given the distinction of firstness. In this view of life, a person finds their value in their connection to other people. If you are needed and valued, you matter. If you aren't and don't, you are nothing. Among others, this is a super-popular option for moms, for people whose self-worth is too low for pure selfishness to be much of an option, and for anybody who finds themselves willfully circling a person or group who enjoys some kind of celebrity status.

But alas, other-centered-ness ultimately yields no more benefit than self-centeredness. The bottom line is that if your number one priority is other people, you may never be bored, but you will always be empty.

So let's demote people entirely for a while and try elevating some other thing that exists in the broad category of Everything Else. Let's see how life works when stuff is given number one priority.

Some people are car people, meaning that they like cars. Other people are car people meaning that their car is literally the most important thing in their life. It is what they work for. It is what they spend their free time with. It is what they talk about. It is what they live for.

Now take the word "car," substitute it for any of a million other possibilities, and you have a glimpse into the world of stuff-centeredness. Some people are sports people. Some people are job people. Some people are politics people. You get how this works.

I was at a motorcycle rally once in which I witnessed a relatively slow-speed motorcycle accident. The leather-vested driver of a motorcycle managed to zig when he should have zagged, and a split-second later his motorcycle was sliding sideways in one direction while he was sliding in the other and an unfortunate young woman on the back of his motorcycle was sliding in yet another direction.

But that wasn't the worst part.

The worst part happened when the road-rashed biker leapt to his feet and ran *not* to the aid of his wounded female passenger as she lay on the pavement, but to his motorcycle.

Welcome to the wide world of stuff-centeredness. A worldview in which the things that you have define who you are. A world in which a human being bleeding on the ground is less important than a motorcycle lying on its side.

But before we all collectively eye-roll that hapless, sleeveless biker into the You-Have-Got-to-Be-Kidding-Me Hall of Fame, let's acknowledge a powerful truth: Stuff-centeredness offers a tremendously tempting hope that self-centeredness, other-centeredness, and even God-centeredness do not.

Stuff-centeredness offers the possibility of control. And you know that you like control.

In a self-centered world you get the illusion of all-importance. In an other-centered world you get to be a savior. But in a stuff-centered world you get the illusion of control.

Motorcycles never talk back. Neither does money. Neither does alcohol, food, or narcotics. Neither does a perfectly organized house. Neither does porn.

That makes you the boss. An imaginary boss in a very tiny universe. But still, the boss. And when your life is screaming your failure and unworthiness into the echoing emptiness of your soul, sometimes inventing a tiny world in which you are the boss feels like very good medicine.

Take a second and check your phone. You probably already have since the average person checks their phone about every five minutes or so. But take a second and check again.

Now remember our two categories of being: God and Everything Else.

Which category is filling your life? God, or Everything Else?

Let's just say that your life is so full today that you feel like somebody duct-taped your lips around a garden hose and then slowly turned on the water. As you are drowning in the stuff of your life, would it be more accurate to say that you are drowning in God today, or drowning in Everything Else?

For most of us, there is no question which of

those two categories fills more of our lives.

Back at that storming desert mountain, there were no smartphones. In fact, even calendars and to-do lists as we know them hadn't been invented yet. As the presence of God raged on that mountain, there was (by our standards) very little to distract the people gathered below. Their job was to eat the food that God provided for them, drink the water that God provided for them, and wait.

But they couldn't do it.

They could not live in the shadow of God as He was beginning to unfold the story of Everything to their leader on the mountain top. Rather than accept that position, they chose to huddle in the shadow of God Almighty and create a fake god that they could control. Seriously.

That was a very bad idea. For extra credit you can read about it in the Book of Exodus, Chapter 32, but that's more like page 76 of the Bible, so we're not going to talk a lot about it here. I mention it because I want to introduce a word to you that we have to talk about if we are going to wrap our heads around the firstness of God and the not- first-ness of Everything Else. The word is idolatry. It's an ancient word that means *treating something that is not God like it is God.*

From this perspective, idolatry is the right word to describe what happens any time we take anything from the category of Everything Else and give it firstness.

The second most important thing you need to know about idolatry is that it doesn't work. We just saw that in Exodus, Chapter 32. No matter what other thing you make the most important thing in your life, you will still be empty.

The most important thing you need to know about idolatry is that God doesn't like it. You can finish your extra credit assignment to discover how much.

Again I ask you: what is filling your life today? God, or Everything Else?

BECAUSE GOD IS FIRST, YOUR LIFE HAS ORDER

God is first.

As your life fills to the brim, crashes like an ocean wave, and then begins to refill again, there could not be better news than this. Right here, in this one three-word sentence derived from the first words of the first page of the Bible, life begins to find order, structure, and clarity.

Right here, we start to understand how it is that we can try so hard and still be so empty.

We are empty because our lives are out of order.

Then, because our lives lack their designed order, they become overly full with things that should never be there in the first place. And then, because our lives are disordered and over-filled, we lack all sense of clarity. In this state of overwhelmed confusion, there is nothing left but to keep doing whatever we have done to keep trying to fill our empty souls from the outside in.

Well, almost nothing.

There is this one bright hope. As our lives buzz and ding and push and pull us ever onward toward the next scenic overlook of what might have been, we could stop. Just stop.

In this brief pause, we could acknowledge the insanity and absurdity of a life so devoid of *something* that it is filled with *everything*.

Seriously, this is crazy.

A life so untethered and swept away that it requires a pocket-sized computer a thousand times more powerful than the one that landed men on the moon to offer up several hundred reminders every day that this life isn't working.

And finally, having acknowledged the frazzled, insane absurdity of it all, we can go back to that mountain. That terrifying mountain, set upon by the

LORD of all creation.

And from there, quaking in the shadow of the fire and the fury, we can choose to accept a world-changing, life-shattering truth.

God is first.

And not by a little, as if He were the first grain of sand to pass through an hourglass. God is first by a margin as incomprehensible as it is infinite. God is first because God is only. There is nothing else like Him. He is the source of everything. Apart from Him there is nothing. He is all-powerful, all-knowing, all-seeing, all-everywhere, all the time.

God is first. And because God is first, your life has order.

If God is not first, you'd better be the world's greatest genius because there are and always will be a million rotten things expertly trying to sneak into your life. They will flatter you and fool you on the way in. They will frustrate and falsify your life as they take root. Then they will fling wide the back door of your soul to invite their friends and foment rebellion against any part of you that still remains true. And even if you were the world's greatest genius, you still wouldn't stand a chance.

But God is first. And that means that there is an order of life that actually brings life and makes sense, and you can have it. When God is first, the lies that you believe and the parts of your life that do not belong begin to stick out like a skunk in a room full of kittens. You can see them from a mile away, and you can smell them even when they manage to hide.

Blue, Blue, Banana, Blue. People are masterful pattern finders. And when your life comes into order, all of those God-given parts of your heart and mind that feel the burden of the confusion of an un-ordered life will kick into gear on a whole new level and you will daily discover the parts of your life that are out of order. You will see them for what they really are. You will avoid new ones like a ballerina in a dodgeball tournament. And you will celebrate as you throw old and entrenched behaviors and beliefs off the back of your train.

God is first. If it matters, it flows from Him. If it does not flow from Him, it does not matter.

Because God is first, your life has order.

And now prepare to hear the chains of your life go clattering to the floor.

BECAUSE GOD IS FIRST,
YOU ARE FREE

I f God is not first, your life is an impossible patchwork of obligation and isolation in which you are simultaneously enslaved to masters who care neither about you nor each other. If God is not first, you are doomed to waste your days fluttering from meaningless obligation to meaningless obligation while trying to steal the occasional moment of rest via a mindless romp through your social media account or a trip to Branson.

But God *is* first. And that means that every ounce of obligation and consternation that drives you to waste your life in pursuit of things that are not from God is nothing more or less than phony. It is not real. Therefore it has no power over you. Because God is first, you are free.

From all of the guilt of a lifetime of not being what your so-called masters say you're supposed to be: free. From all of the fear of failing to be and do all of the things that an invaded, infected, and overwhelmed life requires you to be and do: free. From all of the pressure to be great and all of the shame of being so much less: free. From all the lies that promise you a better tomorrow, or at least a better today: free. Because God is first, you are free.

Take that, chains.

BECAUSE GOD IS FIRST,
YOU HAVE CLARITY

I f God is not first, you are guaranteed all the clarity offered by a smeared and bug-splattered windshield as you drive directly into the sun. Do or don't? Stay or go? Yes or no? You can add these to a very long list of questions to agonize over until you finally give up altogether and live your life with all of the intentionality of a jellyfish, forever doomed to float with the current, take whatever comes your way, and pretend it's what was meant to be.

If God is not first, there is no such thing as clarity because there is no such thing as clear. There is only the darkness of a blindfolded life that craves the sun.

But God is first. And He literally invented the sun.

Imagine yourself drifting in the proverbial soup of life. The sights and sounds and smells all begin to merge together. Yes becomes maybe, then no, then maybe again. Years pass, and the thing that most of those years have in common is that *you don't know what to do.*

Now imagine yourself standing on a sidewalk with no idea if you should continue forward or turn around and go back. You close your eyes. As you stand there, seeing nothing, you feel the sun warm your face. You remember that your whole life is happening on a very small area of the surface of one planet.

You remember that the Sun is 93 million miles away and yet so huge and hot that even though it takes a ray of light seven full minutes to travel from the Sun to Earth, the heat of the Sun can actually burn your flesh. You remember that the Sun is a mediocre star among 300 billion others in the galaxy. You remember that the galaxy is one of 300 billion others estimated to exist in the universe.

And you remember that all of that exists because

on page one of the Bible, God said, "Let there be light."

Suddenly, the soup of life isn't so soupy. You have the light of an absolute truth to shine into any situation.

Because God is first, you have clarity.

BECAUSE GOD IS FIRST, NOTHING ELSE IS

The first truth that we find on page one of the Bible is that God is first. And in that truth we find freedom, order, and clarity for our real lives right now. The firstness of God is a truth of such gravity that it has the power to reshape your entire life, starting right in this moment.

What are the things that come first in your life? Take some time and write them down. And be honest. Lying to yourself is like lying to your doctor. You can do it, but it's not going to help anything.

Most probably, one of the things that you put

first in your life sometimes is you. A bunch of the crazy in your life might be grounded in this simple and common act of disorder. You want what you want, and in some moments that is the most important fact in your life. And it is also an act of idolatry because it is you stealing the crown of God's firstness and trying to place it on your own head. Bad plan.

I remember a time when I did that.

Ok, I remember lots of times when I've done that, but I'm going to tell you about one. I was in my early twenties, and my life was on a definite upswing. I was newly married, excelling at my job, and things were grand. We had just moved to a new city. I had transferred to a different office at work and received a big performance bonus. We moved from an ancient, smoke-befouled four-plex in our old town into a nice new urban apartment. In our old four-plex, our furniture consisted of a few wicker chairs. We filled our new apartment with brand new furniture, the fruits of my big bonus at work.

So I would come home at the end of another productive workday to my beautiful wife in our classy apartment, and I would sit down with our beautiful fluffy cat in my brand new leather recliner. And as I sat there surveying my little one-bedroom kingdom (with fireplace!), I would say to myself, "I have done this."

And that was the moment.

In that moment, I was committing an act of idolatry. Though I have never spoken the universe (or anything else) into existence, in that moment I was claiming firstness over God. And not because I had solved world hunger or initiated world peace. Because of a chair.

It is a bad plan to give firstness to yourself.

Another bad plan is to give firstness to other people. That happens sometimes as a mis-expression of love. We think somebody is so great that our universe begins to revolve around them. Be they a screaming rock star, a smiling and beguiling love interest, or a screaming newborn, that's a bad plan. And not only is it bad for us, it's bad for them. No one can wear the crown of God's firstness. It does not work for us to take it upon ourselves, and it is not ours to give to another.

But sometimes it's not misguided love that motivates us to give firstness to other people. Sometimes it happens because we lack the courage to take responsibility for our own lives. So we keep elevating somebody else so we can give our lives to them. Though the phony promises and real pain of this particular approach are different than the first, the end result is the same. Bad plan.

Our final refuge of rejecting God's firstness is giving firstness away to something else. If your life is dictated more by golf than God, this is you. If you can substitute the word "golf" for any other word and make this sentence true, this is you. If you have a chemical or behavioral addiction, this is you.

In every case, this is not the *whole story* of you. That's important. Everybody has their own hand-crafted way of weaving a story in which these parts of us are discreetly painted over. In fact, the more committed you are to your idolatry or addiction, the more committed you are to making excuses about it. So yes, I am certain that you have your reasons. God knows I do, and if we were having this conversation in person I would undoubtedly have compassion for that.

But we're not.

From here you are just an idea to me and I am only words on a page or screen to you, so I'm going to take advantage of that distance to offer up some frank advice. If ever and why ever you ever steal the crown of God's firstness and put it on anything other than God, you are making a terrible mistake that is destroying your life.

And the glorious opposite side of that coin is that if right now you are willing to surrender yourself and your life to this simple truth that God is first, then there is freedom and order and clarity waiting for you that will forever change your life.

And that's the first truth:

God is first.

THE SECOND TRUTH

Everything Else

P age one of the Bible starts with God, because He is first. What happens next is Everything Else.

In an act of indescribable power and order and artistry, God goes about the business of creating Everything Else. And I warn you from the beginning, as you read the rest of page one of the Bible, you are in great danger of missing the point.

In the beginning God created the heavens and the earth. Now the earth was formless and empty, darkness was over the surface of the deep, and the Spirit of God was hovering over the waters.

And God said, "Let there be light," and there was light. God saw that the light was good, and he separated the light from the darkness. God called the light "day," and the darkness he called "night." And there was evening, and there was morning—the first day.

And God said, "Let there be a vault between the waters to separate water from water." So God made the vault and separated the water under the vault from the water above it. And it was so. God called the vault "sky." And there was evening, and there was morning—the second day.

And God said, "Let the water under the sky be gathered to one place, and let dry ground appear." And it was so. God called the dry ground "land," and the gathered waters he called "seas." And God saw that it was good.

Then God said, "Let the land produce vegetation: seed-bearing plants and trees on the land that bear fruit with seed in it, according to their various kinds." And it was so. The land produced vegetation: plants bearing seed according to their kinds and trees bearing fruit with seed in it according to their kinds. And God saw that it was good. And there was evening, and there was morning—the third day.

And God said, "Let there be lights in the vault of the sky to separate the day from the night, and let them serve as signs to mark sacred times, and days and years, and let them be lights in the vault of the sky to give light on the earth." And it was so. God made two great lights—the greater light to govern the day and the lesser light to govern the night. He also made the stars. God set them in the vault of the sky to give light on the earth, to govern the day and the night, and to separate light from darkness. And God saw that it was good. And there was evening, and there was morning—the fourth day.

And God said, "Let the water teem with living creatures, and let birds fly above the earth across the vault of the sky." So God created the great creatures of the sea and every living thing with which the water teems and that moves about in it, according to their kinds, and every winged bird according to its kind. And God saw that it was good. God blessed them and said, "Be fruitful and increase in number and fill the water in the seas, and let the birds increase on the earth." And there was evening, and there was morning—the fifth day.

And God said, "Let the land produce living creatures according to their kinds: the livestock, the creatures that move along the ground, and the wild animals, each according to its kind." And it was so. God made the wild animals according to their kinds, the livestock according to their kinds, and all the creatures that move along the ground according to their kinds. And God saw that it was good.

Then God said, "Let us make mankind in our image, in our likeness, so that they may rule over the fish in the sea and the birds in the sky, over the livestock and all the wild animals, and over all the creatures that move along the ground."

So God created mankind in his own image,
   in the image of God he created them;
   male and female he created them.

God blessed them and said to them, "Be fruitful and increase in number; fill the earth and subdue it. Rule over the fish in the sea and the birds in the sky and over every living creature that moves on the ground."

Then God said, "I give you every seed-bearing plant on the face of the whole earth and every tree that has fruit with seed in it. They will be yours for food. And to all the beasts of the earth and all the birds in the sky and all the creatures that move along the ground—everything that has the breath of life in it—I give every green plant for food." And it was so.

God saw all that he had made, and it was very good. And there was evening, and there was morning—the sixth day.

Thus the heavens and the earth were completed in all their vast array.

By the seventh day God had finished the work he had been doing; so on the seventh day he rested from all his work. Then God blessed the seventh day and made it holy, because on it he rested from all the work of creating that he had done.
~Genesis 1:1-2:3

It is magnificent.

God speaks, and it happens. Just like that. Even the order of the things that God speaks is magnificent. For example, in days one, two, and three, God creates light, then sky and water, then the dry ground. And then in perfect order in days four, five, and six, he gives shape to the light, then populates the sky and water, then populates the land.

A person could spend their entire life studying these words and discover layer after layer, secret after secret. And as day six unfolds, it becomes clear that on the land is where the most important story is going to be told.

But I think when we read the first page of the Bible, it is hard for us to see the beauty and the majesty. In fact, it's entirely possible that rather than taking a moment to lose yourself in the perfect words of the first page of the Bible, you just skimmed right over them to see what imperfect words I would follow them with.

It's easy for us to do that because many modern readers of the Bible tend to ask only two questions as they read the remainder of the first page of the Bible:

Is evolution a real thing? and, How long did this take?

When we consider cosmology (the origins of the universe), these seem like the two questions we're supposed to ask. And that's fine, from a certain perspective.

The first page of the Bible outlines the creation of the universe. Therefore, it has much information to offer as we seek answers to our modern questions about the age of the universe and the mechanics of how life came to be. In fact, I believe that the Bible should be our primary resource in answering those questions.

But you are not going to find the promised second truth that is going to change your life by trying to unravel the age of the universe and the mystery of life, because those were not the questions that the first page of the Bible was originally written to answer.

Return with me back to the mountain, and let's consider what we can see from there.

BACK TO THE MOUNTAIN

It's hard to be a nobody.

Being a nobody means that nothing about you matters, including what you do and what other people do to you. And for our slave nation gathered and grumbling at the foot of that desert mountain, that was life. Or, at least it had been. Long, long ago one of their ancestors had been somebody. But then everything changed, and for hundreds of years they and their ancestors had all been nobodies.

They were a nation of forced slave labor. They had no legal rights. Their children did not get to go to school. They did not get vacation days. They were born, they worked until they died, and then their children worked until they died. And if ever they had too many children, the masters would murder an entire generation of them with such casual brutality that they might as well have been pulling weeds from a garden.

They were such nobodies that even their genocide was not considered a matter of significance.

That was life. Until the day that God showed up and called an end to it. And if you want to find the second life-changing truth revealed on the first page of the Bible, this is where you have to start. As a nobody.

And for some of us, that's easy.

No one chooses to be worthless. Worthlessness is an attribute that other people choose for you. They choose it for you when they mistreat you. They choose it for you when they ignore you. They choose it for you by the things they say to you and refuse to say to you. They choose it for you when they stand by and do nothing. And those seeds descend into your soul, take root, and grow.

Oh how they grow.

Worthlessness becomes so deeply rooted in you and spreads its canopy so broadly above and around you that soon it is the forest in which you live. You don't even think about it, for the same reason that a fish never thinks about water. It becomes an unquestioned fact of your life, a foundational brick of your worldview.

And from there, it doesn't feel weird anymore when people mistreat you, ignore you, verbally and physically and sexually and emotionally and spiritually abuse you. It doesn't feel weird when others do nothing while these things happen to you. It may not feel good, but it doesn't feel weird.

It feels normal. Like sleeping in the mud and breathing heavily-polluted air feels normal for a kid from the slums of Jakarta. It's just the way of things.

Weird is when somebody cares about you.

Weird is when God shows up, grabs your oppressors by the throat, and refuses to let go until they let *you* go. Weird is when God walks you out of your life of oppression, promises you an entirely new life, and brings you to a mountain in the desert to teach you that He thinks you are so great that He wants to be the love of your life.

And weird is extremely uncomfortable. Every worthless person knows how to be mistreated, and no worthless person knows how to feel loved.

Into this discomfort, God speaks.

SPOILER ALERT

On page one of the Bible, God introduces Himself as first. There is Him alone, then He effortlessly makes Everything Else. And for worthless people, there is no question where we fit in the order of things:

At the bottom.

Those people gathered around the mountain had lived their lives as slaves in ancient Egypt. In ancient Egypt, life had a very clear order. At the top of all things were the gods, and there were lots of them. The sun was a god. The moon was a god. Various animals were gods. The Pharaohs were gods. Next were the Egyptian people, considered to be superior to all others. And at the very bottom of everything, lower even than house cats, were the slaves. They were born at the bottom of life, they would die at the bottom of life. They did not matter, and nobody cared.

Unless everything they knew was a lie.

At the base of that mountain, with their leader, Moses, nowhere in sight for days and days, as fear and boredom began to distill into anger and regret, two questions had to be ringing, beeping, and buzzing their way through that collected group of people.

The first question, "Who is God?," we have begun to answer. God is first. He is the glorious and all-powerful maker of everything.

But the second question now looms ever larger. Who are we? Why would the God who is first choose to rescue and reveal Himself to a worthless people??

And so on page one, after God identifies Himself, he unfolds all of His creation. He lights the universe. He gives form to the world. He creates the sun and the moon and the stars. He fills the ocean and the sky with life. He fills the land with creatures.

And it is all just stuff. Not a god in there anywhere, except Him.

The sun and the moon? Just objects. The

crocodiles of the Nile, the hawks of the air, and all the other animals worshiped in Egypt? Just creatures.

God is first. His creation is unfolding and being given shape, like a song or a story building towards its climax. Yet all of the so-called gods of Egypt are mere objects and creatures. Important in their way, but not the point of the story. So what must the apex of this grand creation be? If the sun and the moon and the stars in all of their splendor are only background, and all of the animal gods of Egypt only decoration, what could possibly exist as the crowning achievement of Creator God?

Spoiler alert—it's you.

IMAGE AND APEX

Then God said, "Let us make mankind in our image, in our likeness, so that they may rule over the fish in the sea and the birds in the sky, over the livestock and all the wild animals, and over all the creatures that move along the ground."
So God created mankind in his own image,
   in the image of God he created them;
   male and female he created them.
~Genesis 1:26-27

The universe is a big place. And in all of its grand expanse, there is exactly and only one thing that is or ever has been created in the image of God:

us.

And let me tell you, when the nation of people at the base of the mountain first heard these words, nobody saw it coming. If God had placed them at the bottom of the universe, they would have believed it. If God had placed them somewhere in the middle, they would have probably been pleased. But when they discovered the truth that they were nothing less than image-bearers of God, I suspect that their response to that fact was a lot like ours.

They probably just sat there. Just like you are.

If I told you that the most important person in the world was coming to your town, you might look outside for the parade. If I told you that the most important person in the world was coming to your house, you might change your clothes or vacuum. But if I told you that you were the most important person in the world, you probably wouldn't do anything. Some statements are simply more than we can believe.

This is one of those statements.

As a result, even though philosophers and theologians have been poking around on this idea for the last 3,500 years, for the most part we all just go on with our lives.

When a person discovers that there are great truths of the universe waiting to be known, that person might go looking for them. But when a person discovers that one of the great truths of the universe is about them personally, that same person might just shut their eyes.

Especially if they were a slave. Especially if they had been told they were nothing and treated like they were nobody for so long that they had begun to believe it. Especially if the phone was ringing and the TV was blaring and the grass needed mowing. Especially if life was full and they were empty.

But there it is. Every person you have ever known, including you, are nothing less than image-bearers of the living God.

And it is time for you to open your eyes and choose to see it. Not just about them. Also about you.

CREATORS AND CREDIT

You may have never seen the Mona Lisa. You may have never seen the Great Pyramids of Giza. You may have never seen an elephant. But even if you have never seen them, you know what each of those look like because you've probably seen images of them. Pictures. Drawings. Movies. And because you've seen images of these things, you know a little bit about what they are like. You know that the Mona Lisa has a fascinating smile. You know the pyramids are ancient marvels of engineering. You know that elephants have trunks.

Every person is an image of God.

We are not Him any more than an image of a

french fry is lunch. But more than anything else in all of creation, we are *like* Him.

That makes us very, very special. Specifically, that makes *you* very, very special.

An image is special based on two points of distinction: its maker and its content.

If you painted me a picture of your left big toe and sent it to me, I probably wouldn't keep it. It's not personal, I just don't know you that well and I'm not deeply interested in your left big toe (not you, Mom. I mean the other people reading this). In the art world, that painting in my hands would constitute a lose-lose: I'm not all that connected with the maker or the content.

But if you sent me an original painting by Michelangelo or Vincent Van Gogh or even Andy Warhol, I would definitely keep it. Even if it was a painting of their big toe. I would keep it because the maker of the painting would make the painting valuable to me, no matter the content.

Likewise, if you are a good painter, and you painted me a picture of a sailboat, I probably *would* keep it. Even if I don't know you. Because I like sailboats. The content of the painting would make it valuable to me, even if I don't know you personally.

So let's say that you are special to me, *and* you are a great painter. That is a classic win-win situation. If you sent me a painting, I'm keeping it, and I'm loving it.

In the case of you, me, and every person who has ever lived, *we* are the ultimate win-win situation.

First off, our maker is God. The First, the Fabulous, and the Forever King of Everything. He is the chief designer, engineer, artist, and architect of the universe. He is the ultimate maker.

Second, we are the ultimate content. In every person, God has created nothing less than a self-portrait. That is what it means to be created in the image of God. And that puts every person in a class above anything else in the universe.

In addition to all of that, our value skyrockets even higher because no one has ever seen God in all of the fullness of His glory (yet). But if you have ever seen a person, then somehow you know a little bit about what God is like.

That does not necessarily mean that God has fingernails and a strong appetite for good coffee. Or that it is impossible for God to lick his own elbow. When the Bible says that God created people in His own image, I think that it means something deeper than that.

And whatever it means, it's important. We have no idea if the first people had green eyes or blue hair, but the Bible tells us no less than three times in two verses that they were created in God's image by God's very specific intention.

So fast-forward through 66 books of the Bible and all the way to now, and what can that possibly mean about us today?

SECOND

People are second. That is truth number two. In all of the universe, in all of space and time, people are second.

We talked earlier about how all of existence can basically be divided up into two categories: God, and Everything Else. That's true.

But then there is us. We are not God. We are a part of His creation. So that makes us part of Everything Else. But we are very, very different from Everything Else because we are self-portraits of God. In all of Everything, we are utterly unique.

Because of our absolutely unique position as

creations who are part of Everything Else, but creations made in the image and likeness of God, it makes the most sense to think of all of everything in three categories: God, People, and Everything Else.

God is first. People are second. And everything else doesn't even get a medal. Not even a green ribbon for participation. Because everything else is not really a participant at all. From the stars in the sky to sharks in the ocean to silk ties on accountants, everything else essentially functions as the stage upon which the greatest story in the history of the universe is being played out: the story of God and people.

Did you notice on page one that of all the things that God created, the only one that he actually talked to is us? That's because nothing else is listening. We are the apex of creation. Creation is the story of God and people.

So what does it mean to be the second most important thing in the universe? You might want to silence your cell phone for this part.

CRAVING GREATNESS

Everybody wants to matter.

Not everybody wants to be famous (I don't). Not everybody wants to be rich (OK, guilty on that one). Not everybody wants to be powerful (tempting). But everybody wants to matter.

Everybody wants to wake up every morning and know that they are important. In fact, we want it so badly that most of our lives are deeply shaped by one of two responses to our shared craving for greatness.

For some of us, our lives are deeply shaped by the fact that we have given up on greatness. We are like wanderers in the desert dying of thirst. We have chased so many mirages and eaten so much sand that now we only sit and wait to die. We are thirsty. Oh how we thirst. But we no longer chase water. We have given up.

A life of insignificance comes with a unique kind of emptiness. Other things in life matter, but the more important they are, the more of a barrier exists between them and you. For example, you might think that your kids are the greatest thing in the world. But the more you believe that, the more distant you feel from them.

In fact, maybe that's the word that best describes the life of an unimportant person. Distant. Distant at least from important things. Like an old rotten apple core that feels horribly out of place on a Thanksgiving table, but right at home in the garbage.

The strange part is that you don't even really have to think about it. You don't have to wake up in the morning with an overwhelming sense of your own worthlessness. You don't even necessarily have to know that you believe it, or that you have given up on believing anything else. If it's in there, that simple belief will sculpt your life like hot sun on a snowman.

If you are miserable today and doing nothing about it, it's probably in there. If you only feel at home in garbage can situations, it's probably in there. If you're numb or crying right now, it's probably in there.

And it does not have to be. Not for another second.

But before we dig it out, let's cover the other half of humanity.

The first response to our shared common craving for greatness is to give up. The second response is to strive for it.

Many people spend their entire lives striving for greatness.

For these people, work is all they know. They don't just work to pay their bills, they work to matter. Their response to the emptiness of their souls is to never stop trying to fill it. They have to be right. They have to be better. They have to be more.

And nothing is ever good enough.

People who strive for greatness are always working to connect themselves with what has value, and to distance themselves from anything that doesn't. But because they believe that they themselves are not valuable, as soon as they touch something, it's broken in their eyes. Even if they don't know that they think this way about themselves. In fact, people who strive for greatness are often the last people to acknowledge their own internal lack of greatness.

If ever you see a trail of cast-off accomplishments, at the head of it will most likely be a person who is trying desperately to matter while not even knowing that they think they don't.

A trail of houses. Each of which was nice enough, until they had it. A trail of cars, boats, and other toys. Each of which was proof of greatness, until they owned it. A trail of broken relationships. Each person representing the attainment of another level of greatness. Until they were attained.

And it can never stop.

It can be thwarted. Sometimes by bankruptcy, as our need to materially prove our greatness outruns our ability to pay for it. Sometimes by the breaking down of our bodies with age and stress and misuse. And especially by rejection of people who refuse to be somebody else's next accomplishment.

But it never stops. For those who strive to be great, nothing is ever good enough. Most tragically, including the people they love.

If you chase accomplishment like a bloodhound after an escaped prisoner, this might be you. If every new acquisition in your life inexplicably becomes not good enough, this might be you. If you constantly pressure the people in your life to be better, this might be you. If you feel angry and dismissive right now, this might be you.

And it doesn't have to be you. Not for another second.

Sometimes in our craving for greatness we manage to combine these two opposing approaches. Some people bounce back and forth from seasons of striving to seasons of surrender. Some people spent years or even decades striving for greatness before they crashed, burned, and gave up. Some people never stop striving. Some people never stop surrendering. And some people find bizarre ways to do both at the same time.

And it is time for all of it to be over.

Behold this fact of the universe that will change your life forever: you are already great.

You are great because you are second. You are not great because of the things that you do or the things that you own or because of the people you love or the people who love you. You are great because you are created in the image of God.

That means that your greatness is rooted outside of yourself. And that means that you do not have the power to make your greatness or even really to break it. You are great because God has made you great.

That is the first lesson of second-ness. Because people are second, people are great.

BECAUSE PEOPLE ARE SECOND, PEOPLE ARE GREAT

Think about how different your life would be if you accepted your own second-ness. Never again would you feel unworthy. Never again would you accept whatever awful things life hands you and then feel at home in them. Never again would you strive to accomplish greatness.

How amazing is that? Or at least that's what I want to write. But what I'm really thinking is this: How scary is that?

How scary is the prospect of a fact of the

universe rocking your life down to its foundations? What if, from this moment forward, you can never be the same again unless you willfully choose to believe the lie that you don't matter? What if you and every single person you will ever meet are hand-crafted by God in greatness? What if you are great before you ever get out of bed in the morning, and great even if you don't? What if the biggest low-life you know is nothing less than an image-bearer of the living God?

What if, in all the grandeur of the universe, we truly are second?

BECAUSE PEOPLE ARE SECOND, YOU HAVE AN IDENTITY

I dentity is a funny thing. Our essence never changes, but the way we identify ourselves deeply changes our experience of life.

For 12 years I was the Senior Pastor of a church. And it was a big part of my identity. Not only did my work profoundly shape my life and the way that I spent my time, in my case it even changed my name. I became Pastor Mick.

I always felt weird about that. And I felt extremely weird about the Senior Pastor part. But I also really liked it. One of the great things about an identity is that it provides a tagline for your life.

I'm Mick, the Senior Pastor of a church.

With that one sentence people knew instantly what to think about me (rightly and wrongly) and I knew instantly what to think of myself (also rightly and wrongly).

This is Pat, the school teacher. This is Jayden, the addict. This is Riley, the lawyer. See how easy that is? I make up three people, tell you one thing about them, and it is all you need to know. I didn't even give them gender-specific names. I didn't have to. You probably like Pat, have compassion or disgust for Jayden, and respectfully dislike Riley. And it is all so easy. And so completely and utterly wrong.

Imagine a large pier extending from a beautiful tropical beach with a thousand spectacular, multi-million-dollar yachts all lined up side by side. You and 999 other people are each given a yacht. As you spend the following days getting to know your yachts and getting to know each other, you discover that every single yacht is exactly identical, except that every single yacht has a slightly different color of steering wheel. Pardon me, it's a "helm," now that we are all sailors. But

I'm still going to call it a steering wheel.

Recognizing the fact that the only difference between the yachts are the colors of the steering wheels, which ones of us received the better yachts? Which one of us got the very best yacht?

The question seems meaningless.

To say that one multi-million-dollar yacht is better than an identical yacht with a different color of steering wheel seems ridiculous.

But it is in exactly that realm of ridiculousness in which we live our lives.

All people are created in the image of God. That makes us the second most valuable thing in all of the universe behind God Himself, precisely because we are somehow and somewhat like God Himself. We are the multi-million-dollar yachts. And compared to the fact that we are all created in the image of God, the sum total of all our differences is extremely petty. Like the color of a steering wheel.

And here lies our identity problem. Rather than choosing to identify ourselves by the grand truth of who we are and spending our days fearlessly sailing the high seas of life, we spend our days polishing, covering, and comparing our steering wheels.

What a silly way to live.

Because people are second, we have an identity.

Among other things, that means that you don't get to say who I am.

You might want to. But you don't get to. You might like this book and want to say very nice and complimentary things about me. And I appreciate that. Or you might dislike this book so much that you are keeping notes in preparation for writing the world's most scathing one-star review. But either way, even though you are free to say whatever you want, your words have absolutely no defining power over me.

That is true because I am already fully defined.

Specifically, I am created by God in His image. That makes me second. And because God has made me second, no one can make me anything else.

If for some reason you want to make me first, I am still second. If for some reason you want to make me third or 300th, I am still second. If for some reason I want to make myself something else, I am still second.

And the exact same thing is true of you.

We tend to build our view of humanity based on distinction. Who is taller, who is shorter. Who is lighter, who is darker. Who is richer, who is poorer. In our day-to-day lives, we tend to be much more concerned with how other people are different from us rather than how other people are like us. As a result, we tend to make mountains out of our mole hills of distinction and a molehill out of our shared mountain of second-ness.

Not long ago I was riding a small rented motorbike in elbow-to-elbow traffic in a massive city in southeast Asia. It was crowded. It was hot. It was extremely humid. And yet many of the locals were going about their day in long sleeves, long pants, hats, gloves, and masks.

From my outsider perspective, they looked as though they were dressed to avoid frostbite, covering every exposed inch of skin. But when I asked my local friend why everyone was so heavily covered in such a warm climate, his answer surprised me.

The people were heavily covered to avoid getting a sun tan.

In this particular Asian culture, tanned skin implied poverty, because those who survive by working long, hot days in the fields for low wages naturally become very tanned. And conversely, lighter skin implied the wealth and sophistication of a person who spent their days in luxury and indoors.

Page One

In my part of the world, some people pay good money to get a tan. In the other half of the world, people sweat and suffer to avoid one. And all over the world, people are doing what they are doing for the same reason:

To gain the right kind of distinction, and to avoid the wrong kind.

Some people drive cars they can't afford to feel better about themselves and project an image of status to those around them. Others drive jalopies to hide their wealth and minimize their guilt of out-pacing their neighbors.

The truth of us is that we live our lives as if we are trying to become something. We spend ourselves in a concerted effort to define ourselves and to seek a certain kind of definition from others.

Sometimes we do things for others that make us ashamed to look at ourselves in the mirror. Sometimes we do shameful things to others to look more highly upon ourselves in the mirror.

And it is all baloney. It is time to stop comparing steering wheels and to start sailing.

You are second. Therefore, you have a God-given identity. So do I. End of story.

BECAUSE PEOPLE ARE SECOND,

YOU HAVE A JOB TO DO

You have two thumbs and one belly button. But you were not born for thumb-twiddling and navel gazing. Not by a long shot.

To the contrary, you were born to rule the world.

God blessed them and said to them, "Be fruitful and increase in number; fill the earth and subdue it. Rule over the fish in the sea and the birds in the sky and over every living creature that moves on the ground."
~Genesis 1:28

Did you catch the purpose statement in there? Thus far we have focused on the nature of people: we are created in the image of God. But on page one of the Bible, we also find the purpose of people: to rule.

The first people to ever hear these words were slaves. Not only had they never ruled the world, they had never even ruled their own selves. In their entire lives up to that moment they had never been rulers. To the contrary, they had only and always been ruled. Imagine the shockwave that these words must have sent through them. Not only were they the most important of all created beings and second only to God, but also they were the rulers of the world. That's a lot to take in. Maybe it is a lot for you to take in also.

Most of us are not well-schooled in our secondness. Even those of us who were raised to know about the firstness of God were often taught to view ourselves as low and unimportant.

I have an extrovert challenge for you. Especially if you are in a public place, loudly say the following words:

"I was born to rule the world!"

Almost nobody did that. You probably didn't so much as whisper those words even if you are the only person within hearing distance. To say that phrase aloud feels less like an extrovert challenge and more like an insanity test. It feels like the ranting of an egomaniac.

But congratulations to those of you who pulled it off.

Because it is absolutely true. You might be a slow reader, a low producer, a bad cook, and a worse friend. But you were born to rule the world. Not because you are first. From that deception comes every kind of self-centeredness and arrogance. Because you are second.

Because people are second, we are called to a very unique kind of ruling, an exercise of authority that is classically known as stewardship.

In the ancient world and up until recent times, a steward was a person entrusted to rule the affairs of another person. Imagine an ancient Greek city-state, complete with walls and soldiers and long-boats and trade routes. Between domestic duties, foreign policy, and everything in between, the ruler of a city-state had a very difficult job. So the leader would choose extremely trusted people to rule over parts and pieces of the city-state for him so that the ruler didn't have to. Those people were the stewards.

A more modern example would be managers.

When I was a kid, my idea of the perfect restaurant was Chuck-E-Cheese. It might be the case that one person owned every single Chuck-E-Cheese. But even if that is true, one person did not operate every single Chuck-E-Cheese. Each individual restaurant had a manager. A steward.

In human terms, stewards become important when one person can't do all the work. One king can't rule a large kingdom, so they choose stewards to help them so that the king has time to do things like sleep, shop for cool fur-lined capes, and hopefully take his kids to Chuck-E-Cheese.

But God is not like that. God is first on a completely different level than even the greatest of kings. Remember, this is the God who invented and created the entire universe just by talking in short sentences. God does not need a steward. And He most certainly does not need several billion of them.

And yet, God made people second, and He made them to rule. So what is the deal with that?

Some people like to talk like they know what God was thinking when He did or said certain things. I'm not one of those people.

I know that God made people second, because He said so. Likewise, I know that God made people to rule, because He said so. But *why* He made people to rule even though He obviously does not need the help? I have no idea.

Here is my guess as to why God made people stewards: because He wanted to.

That's it.

I think that God is the all-knowing, first-over-everything Creator. So when He created us in His image, I think He knew that we would need something to do.

And because He wanted us to know Him and be connected with Him, He created a place for us in the family business.

He didn't make us rulers because He was unable or uninterested in ruling the world. If that were the case, He would have needed to give us power over things like death and the laws of physics. Then we might have had a fighting chance of ruling the universe without His intervention. But He didn't.

He made us second and stewards because He wanted us to be able to work with Him. He wanted us to share with Him in the ruling of the universe.

Isn't that fun?

Because people are second, you have a job to do.

BECAUSE YOU ARE SECOND, YOU MATTER

I am so done with trying to look important to other people. And I am so done with other people trying to look important to me. I'm tired of finding ways to slide my accomplishments into conversation in a vain attempt to gain approval, and I'm tired of hearing other people's resumes for the same reason. I'm tired of the anxiety that comes with feeling inferior, and the smug sense of superiority that comes with feeling superior.

And all of it could just go away.

The anxiety and self-righteousness, the name

dropping and resume building, the winning and losing, and the isolation that comes with both. All of it could just go away if we could snuggle up to this simple fact: because we are second, we matter.

Our importance is not derived from who we know or what we do. Our importance is rooted in what we are. We are image-bearers of the Lord God Almighty. Our importance is grounded in the importance and magnificence of God. Because God matters infinitely, we also matter.

I

BECAUSE PEOPLE ARE SECOND, WE ARE ALL EQUAL

Radical equality is a hard pill to swallow. I don't know why I want to be better than you, but sometimes I do. And I don't know why it bothers me so much when you appear to be better than me, but sometimes it does. And this is not a new problem.

Remember, back at the mountain of God, God's people had been culturally defined for generations. They were slaves. Pretty much everything you needed to know about them was wrapped up in that one sentence. Whatever the dog pile of their world looked like, they were at the bottom of it.

And you know exactly who is at the top and bottom of the dog pile of your world.

An interesting fact about people is that we are not remarkably good at ordering most things. If I gave you 30 different glasses of water with 30 different amounts of salt in them and I asked you to taste them and put them in order from most salty to least salty, that would take a lot of work from you and your results probably wouldn't be exact. Likewise if I gave you pictures of 30 different cars and I asked you to put them in order from most to least luxurious, it would take a lot of work and you and your neighbor would put those cars in very different orders.

But if I gave you a list of 30 different people in your community and asked you to rank them by social standing, you'd nail it. It wouldn't be hard, it wouldn't take long, and your list would very closely match up with the list of any other person in your community. The web of social standing is vastly more complex than the quality distinctions among cars. The web of social standing is almost infinitely more complex than ordering the relative saltiness of water. Yet salt water and cars confuse us, and social standing somehow makes perfect sense.

Isn't that interesting? Most people are not good at ordering most things, yet everybody in any community knows who fits where.

And we are absolutely and utterly wrong.

First God. Second people. Then everything else. This is the true order of the universe. And within our secondness, God provides no distinction. Rich people are not more second than poor people. Light people are not more second than dark people. Men are not more second than women. Masters are not more second than slaves.

People are second, and we are all second together. How different would the world be tomorrow if we all chose to live by this one truth today?

BECAUSE WE ARE SECOND, WE HAVE SOMEONE TO THANK

T o the extent that we are thankful at all, we tend to associate thankfulness with what we have. We are thankful for food, friends, and the farm. And that's fine. But there is much more to the story than that.

In addition to being thankful for what we have, we have much cause to be thankful for what we *are*. Not just everything is second. Only we are. Every day we share the experience of being a creation that is like the Creator. We are made from dirt, yet made to commune with the living God.

No person would rather be a bug, or a bear, or a baseball bat. Sometimes we talk like that, but nobody really means it. We may desire the simplicity that we ascribe to a different kind of being, but none of us want to surrender our minds and wills in favor of being an un-reasoning animal or a non-reasoning plant, insect, or object.

Yet it is easy to never really be thankful. Some days we have an overly acute awareness of the things that are wrong with us. And as such, we regularly forget to be thankful that we are us. But we should be. To be us is to be the reflection of glory. Arthritic, stinky-footed glory possibly, but glory nonetheless.

And as we grow in thankfulness, we should not only increase our thankfulness for what we have and what we are, we should remember that we have someone to be thankful *to*.

God literally made us. He is the source of all of our blessings, the source of our place in the universe, and the source of our very selves. We would be wise to make Him the intentional recipient of our thanks.

Can you believe that He would do this for us? Every breath that brings air into our lungs, every heartbeat that pumps the blood of life through our bodies, every thought that leaps through our minds, every emotion that brings fullness to our lives and a tingle to our bodies. Any one of these is an echo of our creation in the image of God. We have cause to live each moment of our lives as a sort of Christmas morning experience.

Because we are second, we have much to be thankful for.

BECAUSE WE ARE SECOND, WE HAVE ZERO CAUSE FOR ARROGANCE

I f pride comes before a fall, then we as a culture must be teetering on the edge of the tallest overhanging cliff in the history of metaphors while a raging river of reality erodes its base. For us, self-exaltation is practically an art form. And even those of us who try not to personally practice it still find ourselves under the sway of people whose primary contribution to the world is nothing more than their own self-promotion.

Page One

A large percentage of the buzzing and dinging of life happens as self-promoters demand your attention as they once again try to demonstrate how much better they are than you. Another large percentage happens as you try to prove them wrong.

But the fatal flaw of self-exaltation is that it requires the claiming of glory.

"Look how great I am! See what I have done!"

These statements and others like them are the clarion calls of pridefulness in all of its forms.

And there is a reason why our arrogance is killing us. There is a reason why it is so hard to keep both ourselves and other people convinced of how first we are.

Because we aren't first. We are second.

Let's say somebody built a robot capable of building a stone wall. Upon the completion of the stone wall, who deserves the credit? The robot, or its builder?

Let's say somebody made a submarine to explore the depths of the ocean. As the ocean is explored, who deserves the credit? The submarine, or its designer?

God built us. And He built us for greatness. So when we accomplish great things, who deserves the credit? The person, or their Creator?

Another word for credit is glory. And glory flows through all of creation. But nothing in creation is designed to hold on to it, especially not us. As the most special and important thing that God ever created, we have a very unique relationship to God's glory. As far as we are aware, no other created thing has the capacity to be amazed. In all of the universe, we are the only beings who can look back out into the universe on a clear and cloudless night and say, "Wow."

Because we are second, we have the ability to experience glory and to be overwhelmed. We marvel when a giant iceberg calves into the sea. We stand in awe beneath a stormy high plains sunset. We laugh when a newborn deer wobbles across a meadow. We gape at the sight, sound, and rumble of an exploding volcano. Because we are second, *we can see glory!*

And because we can experience glory, we can celebrate its Source. Because God made everything, then all glory belongs to Him. It is that simple.

Most everything that we would call glory comes to our senses via some other created thing. But that glory does not belong to the thing because that thing does not belong to itself. Further, that thing most certainly did not create itself. Therefore, all the glory radiating through the world has an owner. It ultimately belongs to God because He made it.

Here is where things really start to get good.

BECAUSE WE ARE SECOND, WE CAN WORSHIP

Because we can experience glory, we can give credit to God for it. Most people call the act of giving credit to God worship. You can call it that too, if you want. But whatever you call it, we should all do it. We shouldn't just say, "Wow, that was cool." We should say, "Wow, God, that was cool."

That may seem like a small distinction, but it isn't. When we say, "Wow, that was cool," we are acknowledging glory, and that's a good thing. But when we say, "Wow, God, that was cool," we are giving God the credit that He deserves both for making something glorious, and for making us able to experience that glory. And if you think about it, the fact that we can experience glory is itself glorious.

And that rabbit hole of glory never stops.

As we begin to give God credit for His glory, we find more glory to give Him credit for. And as that continues, you might just find yourself becoming one of those people who are less and less wrapped up in the buzzing and dinging frustrations of life, and becoming more and more convinced that the world for all of its messes is wonderful and amazing and that life as the second greatest thing in all the universe is the greatest privilege that could ever be given.

Wow, God, that is cool.

Worship. When we begin to live out that one simple act, our entire world begins to fall into place. I'm not talking about singing songs at church, by the way. That *can* be worship, certainly. But worship as a category is vastly broader than that. In fact, as you learn to do this thing called worship, even if you find singing a few songs at church to be beyond boring, you might just discover that you have a glory super power. Because you are second, you were not only created, you also have the power to create. Not only can you recognize glory in things, you can make things.

Maybe you specialize in large granite monuments. Maybe you specialize in pancakes. Maybe you specialize in well-timed kind words. In all three, there is a unique type of glory. And when you create things like these, you also create glory!

You—normal, distracted, you—with less-than-fresh breath or a pinky finger that doesn't work quite right or both. You can create glory. You can create glory through self-sacrifice and everyday kindness and in a hundred other ways in which everybody should participate. And you can create glory in extremely unique ways that are specific to you and you alone. In fact, if your mind is firing with ideas and your heart is warming with excitement as you read these words, you're doing it right now.

You can create glory. But you can't keep it.

Wise is the person who accomplishes great things and then gives God the credit. That person is living their life according to the true order of things. And that person will always have more peace and more confidence in their own value than someone who chooses the way of arrogance.

All glory belongs to Him who is first. Even the glory that you create. In fact, especially the glory that you create. And when you pass it on to God, you commit an act of double worship. First, you create glory. Then, you give that glory to God because He deserves it.

Take a picture in your mind of those dry and empty places inside of you. If you choose to build your life around making glory and giving it to God, all those places are about to be gushing with fullness.

Welcome to the glory cycle. Welcome to a life of worship. Welcome to life.

THE

FOREVER-CHANGED LIFE

THE END OF THE QUEST

For much of my life, well-meaning people told me to go out and make something of myself. And then they congratulated me after I did.

They were wrong.

In fact, they were doubly wrong. And so was much of my life as I climbed and clawed my way toward the top of this particular mountain of meaning.

As I lived out my version of making something of myself, I discovered that this particular mountain, and especially its peak, were a mirage. That was not a truth I wanted to believe. But it was inescapable.

No matter what I accomplished and no matter who noticed, I still felt like a nobody. But there was always more to accomplish. Another degree to gain. Another person to impress. Another dollar to make. Another good thing to do.

So I kept climbing. As if there is something more to life than being an image-bearer of God and the most important thing in all of creation, I kept climbing.

And for the longest time, I honestly thought I would get there. I honestly believed that one day I would wake up and be accomplished. One day I would have made something of myself, and then things would be different.

And for the longest time, I thought that the emptiness in my soul would be filled by this magical entity: accomplishment. One day some kind of hidden gate would open, all of the fullness of my life would wash away the emptiness in my soul, and there I would be. The Reverend Mickey Shane Thornton. Accomplished Person.

And then my life would undergo a miraculous transformation. Suddenly, instead of being an empty person with a full life, I would be the opposite. I would wake up every morning as a full person with an open calendar, all my days pre-purchased by the accomplishments of yesterday. And then I would live the remainder of my days having climbed the mountain of accomplishment, ascended its peak, and taken my place as a somebody who had done something.

Maybe you are like me and you believe your version of that, too.

Or maybe accomplishment is not the lie that you buy into. Maybe for you the lie is acceptance. Maybe it's something else.

But almost certainly you have spent much of your life climbing and clawing after it, then quitting, then starting again. Just like me. Just like most people.

But in the two simple truths that we find on the first page of the first book of the Bible, the unholy quest to become something is ended.

The truth is that we are already something. The truth is that no one has ever made themselves anything. The truth is that God is first, and people are second.

So how do you live in that world? What do you believe, what do you feel, and what do you do with yourself?

From here, it's time for a new quest.

THE NEW QUEST

Eventually, the slave nation left the mountain. But they didn't leave as slaves. They left as the people of God. And before they left, God had already begun to reveal their new life's mission.

They were going to be His people.

That's it. Their identity and their quest were exactly the same. To live out their identity in every part of their lives and experience life with God in such a profound way that people from every tribe and tongue and nation would come and marvel at God and His people.

Their quest was to be a light to the world, reflecting the glory of the unseen God so brightly that the entire world would be drawn to look and to say, "Wow, God, that is cool."

Our quest is essentially the same.

God is first. People are second. And almost nothing about the world in which you live reflects those truths. But you can.

You can choose to live in reality, even in the midst of a world unhinged from it. You can put God first even if others don't even notice Him. You can put people second even as others treat them (and you) like objects to be used and discarded. And when you commit these acts of truth and glory, you become the light. And all who hear of you are drawn to look and are challenged to say, "Wow, God, that is cool."

That is the new quest. The old quest, the one that most people spend their entire lives chasing, is a quest to find meaning by becoming somebody.

The new quest is to live out the fact that you are already somebody. To live under God's firstness and live out your own secondness.

THE FIZZLE THAT STARTED
THE FRAZZLE

They blew it.

The slave nation was so well-adapted to their slavery that they wore the freedom of God like barbed-wire underwear. The truth of God was life-giving and perfect, but they were so misshapen and malformed that it chafed and poked them until they hated it. Even as God was visibly present with them in the desert, time and again they rejected Him.

And for the next 3,500 years, the scope of history took on a repeating cycle. Time and again God would call His people back to Him and the true and faithful life that He built them for.

And time and again the people said no.

Then they died, and their children said no. Then *their* children said no. And then there was you.

So what do you say?

Because everything is created by God, everything shines bright with glory. But there is also darkness. Profound darkness. Because something has gone terribly wrong since the moments recounted on page one of the Bible. In fact, people didn't make it very far before things went wrong. It happens on page three.

In a nutshell, people have rejected God. And after we got that wrong, everything else followed that trend.

As a result, in all of life, the truth of God is deeply obscured. Our daily lives tell us time and again that God does not exist and that people do not matter. Life flashes brightly and constantly with a false light that distracts, dismays, and disillusions us even as the never-ending sounds of our dinging, clanging, calling world deaden our resolve and diminish our hope.

Blinded and deafened to the truth written into the fabric of the universe, people steal God's glory for themselves and create things that are so far from glorious that they can only be called evil. Disconnected from the truth that God is first and people are second, drowning in the disordered lives that follow, people claim the glory of God for themselves.

In this darkness, a little glory for me makes me seem a little better than you. And something sick inside of all of us makes us want to be a little better than somebody else. So when confronted with glory but blinded to the firstness of God and the secondness of people, we claim the glory of God as our own and use it as a platform to stand over and upon our brothers and sisters.

But glory is like radioactive uranium. Handled properly, it can bring all manner of benefit to our lives. But if you try to hoard it for yourself and wear it around like jewelry, it will make you sick, and eventually, it will kill you.

And this is our condition. Sick, dying, and addicted to what is killing us.

Yet in the midst of this darkness, your glorious act of stewardship is to simply be yourself.

You are called and commanded to put God first. You are called and commanded to put people second.

And God help us, we can't.

TURNING THE PAGE

God is first. People are Second. God wrote these truths into the fabric of the universe. And people up to this very moment are trying to either scrub them away or stay too distracted to notice.

That seems like a weird place to end. But that is exactly where page one ends. With God being right and His most glorious creation about to choose wrong. God's chosen glory reflectors (people) have become glory deflectors. And the universe is broken.

But you already knew that.

You already knew everything was broken. Even if you had never been let down, put down, or beat down, still you would know.

You know because you are second. And because you are second there has always been something inside of you telling you that life as it is does not fit you.

But to know where to go from here, we have to turn the page.

Page one of the Bible tells us how things started. But it was a long time ago and feels a long way from here. It is all true, but built into the eternal firstness of God is a problem that feels absolutely unresolvable.

The problem is that we failed Him.

It wasn't just the people around that mountain that failed Him. It was everybody. And most recently, it was us.

I stole His glory once because of a blue leather recliner. Then I stole His glory again when He made me a gifted preacher. And I will probably steal His glory when somebody tells me that they like this book. I don't want to. But I know that eventually I will. That is my history with God. He gives me glorious gifts, and I skim off the top of his glory like a mob boss extorting the neighborhood dry cleaner.

And then after I fail to put God first, I fail to put people second. I have treated people like objects. I have been invited into the greatest and worst moments of people's lives only to sometimes find myself wishing I wasn't there. Again and again I have viewed people as an inconvenience because they wanted something that I did not want to give, most especially my time and attention.

And I have treated myself just as poorly. The truth that people are second is so distorted in me that I can't get it right even when the person in question is me. Maybe there most of all.

And if I have failed to put God first and I have failed to put people second, then you know the order of my life did not somehow straighten up further down the list. I am a glory-stealer, an image-denier, and a creator of evil. And I can't fix it. Not any of it.

And I'm just one of the team.

You also are a glory-stealer. And an image-denier. And a creator of evil. And you can't fix it either. We are second and broken, but God is first and perfect.

So that means that even though people are the ones who have done all of the breaking between page one and now, only God can do the fixing.

You can go ahead and start smiling now, because, if it were possible, God would be even better at fixing than He is at making.

THE NEXT MOUNTAIN

The next mountain was smaller. More like a little hill on the side of a really big hill, by my reckoning. On the really big hill was a city where people had worshiped and rejected God for a long time. And the little hill outside of town was a place to kill people.

The preferred method of execution at the time was called crucifixion. It involved nailing people by their hands and feet to a large wooden cross and letting them hang there for hours or days until they died. It was excruciating, brutal, shameful, evil, and the perfect example of the kind of thing that people create when they forget that God is first and people are second.

And yet this is the place and the method through which God fixed our problem.

After a few thousand years of raising up prophets and priests who called God's people to return to Him, God did something that even He had never done before. Something that most theologians at the time would have said was impossible.

God sent His own Son to become a person.

The Creator became a part of His creation. Jesus became both first and second at the same time.

It was brilliant.

The problem came from people, so the solution had to come from people. But people could never fix their problems with God. So God sent His Son to become a person so He could fix our problems with God. Brilliant.

I've talked about this thousands of times and on multiple continents, but it never ceases to blow my mind.

The day comes and the glory of God and the evil of people collide at the same place at the same time. On that little hill.

Jesus, both God and a person, gets nailed to one of those crosses. He is subjected by people to the most brutal death the world offers. And at the same time, He takes on Himself all of the wrongs of all of the world.

And He dies.

To the people, He died as an enemy of humanity. But to God, He died to save the people. In that moment He fixed our ultimate problem. In His firstness, He restored our secondness.

And God knows that, even now if we have a part to play, we are going to get it at least a little bit wrong. So He didn't give us a part to play. He only gives us a choice.

Every rotten one of us can simply choose to believe in Jesus and be free.

You should totally do that. Immediately.

As in, right now.

If you were going to choose to believe Jesus, how would you do that? What would you say?

Maybe you know exactly what you would say. Maybe your spirit is already racing ahead of your mind and it is getting said right now. If so, go for it.

If you prefer, here is an example of the kind of thing that you might say. But keep in mind, your honesty with God and your choice to trust Him are the important parts, not these exact words.

God, there are problems in my life and a problem between You and me that I can't fix. And it all comes back to my connection with you.

You are first and you made me to be second. But I treated you like you weren't first. It's not working. You sent Jesus to fix my mess by dying for my sins. You really did that.

So I choose to believe it. I accept the truth that you are first. I accept the truth that people are second. And I accept the gift of Jesus dying for my sins. Wow, God, that was cool. Thank You.

THE NEW TODAY

God is first. We are second. God has already fixed our every failure. We believe Him and we are thankful for it. Now your tiny phone with all of its beeping doesn't stand a chance. In fact, the entire world with all of its deceptions and enticements doesn't stand a chance. Compared to the firstness of God and the secondness of people, all of that other stuff is just... small.

From here, we have a whole new day and a whole new life to live in it. The glory of God is roaring from Earth and sky. Our privilege and our joy is to recognize and celebrate it.

Further, the secondess of people is peering at us from around every corner. In fact, the secondness of people is the reason we even have corners, and houses, and cars, and fields, and every other invention that has previously been such a distraction. We made that stuff. And we are capable of deciding which of the things we have made contribute to the firstness of God and the secondess of people, and which of those things distract us.

We have some hard decisions to make. There are things in our lives that should not be there. Cannot be there. And it's going to be hard to cut them loose. Especially when they keep looking for a way back in. And there are going to be hard days. Maybe lots of hard days. The world is still crosswise with God, even if you aren't. And that can make for a pretty rough life sometimes.

But there is vastly more fullness in a hard true life than in any easy false one.

And you are not alone in this.

There are literally hundreds of millions of people in the world right now who are imperfectly living out the firstness of God and the secondess of people, and you can join them. Choosing to connect your life with a group of others who are trying to live this life together is a decision that will make a huge impact in your life. Find a church like that and jump in. One good resource to find that kind of church is www.efca.org.

Additionally, there are mountains of helpful resources available online and in print designed to help you continue in your connection with God.

The first one to consider is the Bible. If there is this kind of life-changing truth on the *first page*, imagine what else must be in there? And unlike every other resource you will find, the Bible is perfect!

Don't feel bad if the Bible seems confusing and even boring. That is how it feels for most everybody at first. But keep at it. I suggest that you start by reading the Book of Luke, and then the Book of Acts. That will give you a great history of what it was like when Jesus came, and what happened as people around the world started following Him.

Keep in mind that every other resource (including this one) is less important than the Bible, and less than perfect. But they can still be very helpful. My website is micksminute.com, and it is designed for people exactly like you who are looking for the kind of life that God has planned for them. And please reach out to me from there. I would love to answer any questions you may have and hear about how this book or anything else is affecting your life. You will make my day.

Some people have been Christians for a long time, and yet still walk in the emptiness of the kind of life that this book describes. If that is you, that's ok. You are not alone. In fact, you're not even abnormal. But God has so much more for you. Faith in Jesus is transformational. It starts by changing our connection with God. And it's designed to change our connection with everything else also. Our past, present, and future. Let me know how I can help you continue to walk forward into the freedom and new life that God has for you.

I have a lot of words. But if this book helped you make the decision to trust Jesus and follow Him into the life He has planned for you, I do not have words to describe how thrilled I am. I am doing a happy dance in my soul that would break the internet if it could be seen. Please contact me through my website. I want to know. I want to help. I want to happy dance.

Another good resource is Christian radio.

Especially as you drive from place to place and thing to thing, Christian radio is a great way to intentionally fend off the stress and craziness of life, to learn more about God, and to fill your life with the sound of worship. And who knows, you might even occasionally hear one of my "Mick's Minute" broadcasts.

I also strongly encourage you to start helping other people get connected to God and the life He offers us. It's tempting to think that you are not qualified or capable of doing that. But it is always tempting to think that. There is a part of me that is thinking that about myself right now. Check out resources like worldorphans.org and dream of the possibilities that God might have in store for you both in your family and neighborhood, and maybe even around the world! I know some life-changing, world-travelling missionaries of all ages. One thing they tend to have in common is that they never saw this life coming their way. Until it did.

And most important of all, as you walk in the truth of the firstness of God and the secondness of people, God Himself is going to be there for you. Even when you get it wrong, He is going to be there for you. That is His history. Don't feel like your job is to follow

Page One

God without His guidance. It isn't. He has much to say to you, and He wants to hear everything you want to say to Him. Even the kinds of things that you think might bore or even offend Him. Just start talking.

God settled on that mountain and brought His people page one to help them. He was with them in the desert to guide and guard them. He eventually sent Jesus to rescue their souls. And He will be there for you.

Wow, God, that is cool.

THANK YOU

Special thanks to everyone who made this book possible:

—**God.** My Lord and King. You have given me this moment and this calling, and I am so grateful for this privilege. Thank You for making me, making a hope for me, and making a place for me. Truly You are first.

—**My family.** Coming home to you every day is a far greater blessing than anything I do when I am away.

—**The Ainsworth Evangelical Free Church.** Serving as your Senior Pastor for 12 years was one of the defining blessings of my life.

—**Marianne Abel-Lipschutz.** My editor and friend.

—**All the subscribers to www.micksminute.com.** You are a far greater blessing to me than you know.

—**Our financial supporters.** You are the reason I can spend my time helping people connect with God through writing and radio. If you weren't all so modest, I would list your names bigger than mine on the cover of this book.

—**You.** Thank you for taking the time to read this book. As you continue to live out the firstness of God and the secondness of people in your life, I would be honored if you would reach out to me on my website www.micksminute.com and let me know how this book is helping. We have a growing amount of other resources there as well.

I love to help people connect the dots between themselves and God. My prayer is that I have helped you do exactly that. Please let me know if you would like me to come and speak at your church or event, or if you know of a radio station that you think would benefit from my "Mick's Minute" weekly radio show.

And if you would like to support this ministry, there are several ways you can do that:

—Donations through the website are extremely important to this ministry. Every donation buys time that I am able to spend writing and recording rather than working to provide for our financial needs in other ways. If you would like to become a part of this ministry by being one of these "others," I would be honored.

—Taking the time to rate this book on Amazon or other places is a *huge* help.

—Signing up for our email list and sharing the book and our website on social media is a great way to help us connect with more people. It also opens the door for us to send encouragement your way and keeps you in the know about things like my next book!

—Please take a moment to pray for us. Life in ministry is a uniquely complicated experience and I am deeply thankful to God for those who support us with prayer.

ABOUT THE AUTHOR

Mick Thornton is an ordained pastor in the Evangelical Free Church of America who loves helping people connect the dots between themselves and God and hates writing about himself in the third person. He has an undergraduate degree in Political Science from Wichita State University and a Master of Divinity degree from Denver Seminary. He recently concluded a career in pastoral ministry to follow God into a new ministry adventure focusing on writing and radio. His "Mick's Minute" weekly radio show has been heard by listeners across Nebraska and South Dakota for years, and is now gaining an even broader reach. *Page One* is Mick's first book on this adventure with, God-willing, many more to follow. His website is micksminute.com.

Made in the USA
Coppell, TX
03 December 2019

12279034R00099